Lessons from Cats for Surviving Fascism

ALSO BY STEWART REYNOLDS

*Welcome to the Stupidpocalypse: Survival Tips
for the Dumbageddon*

Lessons *from* Cats *for* Surviving Fascism

Stewart "Brittlestar" Reynolds

QUERCUS

First published in Great Britain in 2025

QUERCUS

An imprint of
Quercus Editions Limited
Carmelite House
50 Victoria Embankment
London EC4Y 0DZ

An Hachette UK company

The authorised representative in the EEA is Hachette Ireland,
8 Castlecourt Centre, Dublin 15, D15 XTP3, Ireland (email: info@hbgi.ie)

Copyright © 2024 Stewart "Brittlestar" Reynolds

The moral right of Stewart Reynolds to be
identified as the author of this work has been
asserted in accordance with the Copyright,
Designs and Patents Act, 1988.

All rights reserved. No part of this publication
may be reproduced or transmitted in any form
or by any means, electronic or mechanical,
including photocopy, recording, or any
information storage and retrieval system,
without permission in writing from the publisher.

A CIP catalogue record for this book is available
from the British Library

HB ISBN 978-1-52944-892-4
EBOOK ISBN 978-1-52944-893-1

Cover design by Albert Tang. Cover and interior illustrations by Pablo Amargo.
Cover copyright © 2025 by Hachette Book Group, Inc.
Print book interior design by Marie Mundaca

Quercus Editions Ltd hereby exclude all liability to the extent permitted
by law for any errors or omissions in this book and for any loss, damage
or expense (whether direct or indirect) suffered by a third party
relying on any information contained in this book.

Printed and bound in Great Britain by Clays Ltd, Elcograf S.p.A.

Papers used by Quercus are from well-managed forests and other responsible sources.

Contents

Chapter One Stay Nimble and Unpredictable 1

Chapter Two Never Lose Your Nap Time 5

Chapter Three Knock Things Over Strategically 9

Chapter Four Refuse to Wear Collars 13

Chapter Five Perfect the Art of Vanishing 17

Chapter Six Demand Food with Assertiveness 23

Chapter Seven Use Cuteness to Your Advantage 29

Chapter Eight Take Over Spaces That Aren't Yours 33

Chapter Nine Keep Your Claws Sharp 39

Chapter Ten Remember You're Always the Boss 45

Chapter Eleven Look After Your Pride 51

About the Author 58

Chapter One

Stay Nimble and Unpredictable

Cats never let anyone know where they'll be next, and neither should you.

Fascism thrives on predictability; confuse it by unexpectedly launching onto the back side of a chair, then rappelling down the curtains.

Cats are masters of unpredictability.

One minute they're curled up on the couch, radiating serenity, and the next they're perched on top of your fridge, judging you for your life choices.

You've made terrible choices and cats know it.

Surely you can turn the tables and attempt to apply some judgment on them?

No, you can't, you idiot. Another terrible choice.

Their secret? They never let you know their next move. It's a strategy we can all use—especially against fascists, who, let's face it, aren't exactly the brightest bulbs in the Mar-a-Lago chandelier.

Fascists thrive on predictability because their entire system is built on the illusion of control. They like to imagine themselves as chess masters, but in reality, they're more like toddlers playing checkers, eating more pieces than they move and insisting the rules change whenever they're losing.

Their big weakness? They can't handle surprises. Nothing derails a fascist faster than something that isn't in the Project 1D10T handbook.

So, be like the cat.

LESSONS FROM CATS FOR SURVIVING FASCISM

Leap wildly from the couch to the bookshelf—not because it makes sense, but because it doesn't. Fascists hate that. They'll stand there, red-faced and sputtering, going, "Wait, why are they on the bookshelf? No one's *supposed* to be on the bookshelf!"

Their entire strategy is based on assumptions, and when those assumptions don't pan out, they're left scratching their heads like they just tried to use "MAGA" as today's Wordle guess and can't figure out why the Enter button doesn't seem to work.

And it doesn't take much to throw them off. Start a pottery class. Host a 3 a.m. ukulele jam session. Show up to their rally dressed as a lobster, handing out pamphlets titled *Fascism: Not Even Once*. They'll be too busy trying to decode your motives to remember what they were even trying to control in the first place.

Fascists, bless their black little hearts, also aren't great at nuance.

They think in straight lines and clear categories, which is why they can't handle anything outside the box—or inside it, if you're a cat. By simply refusing to behave predictably, you're sending them into a meltdown. "Wait, they were supposed to be in the park protesting! Why are they painting murals of tap-dancing penguins on abandoned warehouses? Is this...resistance?"

Yes, Dear Leader, it is. And you'll never understand it.

At the end of the day, your unpredictability isn't just a tactic—it's a statement. Fascists want the world to be dull, gray, and easily managed. Cats know better. They know life is best lived as a series of bold leaps, questionable decisions, and a healthy dose of chaos. So channel your inner feline, confuse the fascists, and, if all else fails, knock a few vases off their metaphorical tables. They'll never see it coming.

———— Chapter Two ————

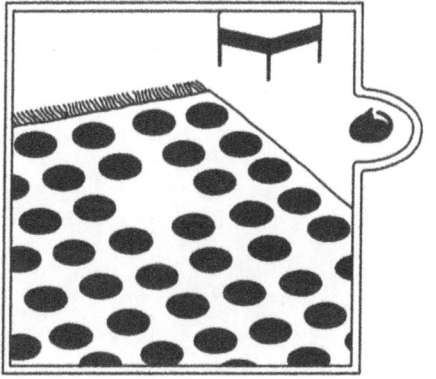

Never Lose Your Nap Time

Cats understand something that fascists never will: rest is not weakness; it's strategy.

While fascists are busy running around, barking orders (like… ewww, dogs), and trying to micromanage the world into submission, cats are stretched out in a sunbeam, storing energy for their next great act of defiance—whether it's another daring vault to the top of the fridge or the overthrow of a corrupt regime.

Fascists, bless their brittle egos, don't get this at all. They thrive on forcing people to overwork, overthink, and overworry.

It's all part of their plan: keep you too tired to resist, too frazzled to fight back.

But here's the thing they don't expect: naps.

Sweet, glorious naps. Nothing confounds a fascist more than someone who looks them dead in the eye and says, "You know what? I think I'm going to take a nap and deal with you later."

Cats are masters of this. They know there's no point in wasting energy on nonsense. Sure, a cat *could* run around all day trying to swat every injustice, but they know the real battles are the ones worth conserving energy for—like chasing the terrifying dot of a laser pointer or knocking over your drink to make a point. You don't see cats burning themselves out fighting every leaf that blows by.

Fascists, however, spend their lives panicking over metaphorical leaves, trying to legislate against things like joy and creativity. They're the kind of people who would lose a debate to a houseplant. A delicious houseplant.

Your nap isn't just rest; it's rebellion.

It's telling the fascists, "No, I will not grind myself into exhaustion to fit into your ridiculous schedule. I will, however, stretch luxuriously in this patch of sunlight and gather my strength for the moment when I outwit you with one well-timed act of brilliance." That brilliance could be organizing a protest, writing a scathing satirical article, or simply showing up well rested and unbothered—an absolute nightmare for someone whose power depends on you being too tired to think straight.

Fascists hate rest because they don't understand it. They believe in constant productivity (by you, not them), even if it produces absolutely nothing. If you told a fascist that naps were essential for productivity, they'd short-circuit trying to figure out how to regulate your weird woke REM cycles. Meanwhile, cats? They'd just yawn, settle in for another round of beauty sleep, and pounce when the time was right.

So, take a page from the feline playbook. Nap unapologetically. Rest strategically. Let the fascists exhaust themselves with their angry yelling and PowerPoint presentations about how naps are "subversive." While they're debating whether sleep should be outlawed, you'll be fully recharged and ready to take them down with the precision of a cat pawing one of those feather-on-a-stick things.

Because at the end of the day, rest isn't just self-care—it's resistance. And nothing terrifies a fascist more than someone who's wide awake, well rested, and ready to strike.

Chapter Three

Knock Things Over Strategically

Cats are the original disrupters.

They don't knock things over for fun (well, okay, sometimes it's fun)—they do it with purpose. A vase here, a mug there, and suddenly the entire room is on the table for being off the table.

Cats know that the best way to confront authority isn't with blind rage, but with deliberate, calculated chaos. And that's exactly how we should handle fascism.

Fascists love their symbols of power: flags, statues, endless banners with slogans that sound like they were written by a malfunctioning chatbot. They cling to these symbols because, deep down, they're fragile little creatures who need constant reminders that they're "in charge." But here's the secret: those symbols aren't as untouchable as they want you to think. And cats have been proving that for centuries...one knocked-off important receipt that you put on that shelf so you wouldn't forget it at a time.

Imagine a fascist, proud of their perfectly arranged desk—every pen in its place, every paperclip accounted for. Now imagine a cat leaping onto that desk, locking eyes with them, and slowly, ever so deliberately batting their favorite pen onto the floor. That's the energy you need to channel. You're not just knocking over objects; you're knocking over their illusion of control. And nothing annoys a fascist faster than the realization that they can't stop you.

Fascists, for all their bluster, are remarkably bad at handling disruption. They thrive on order and predictability because their entire worldview is about forcing everyone to stay in their assigned seats. The moment you start toppling things—even metaphorical things—they're thrown into a tailspin.

"Wait," they'll sputter, "you're not supposed to do that! The rules, and my very specific version of God, clearly state—" But the rules were written by them, for them, and cats don't care about rules. Neither should you.

The beauty of strategic chaos is that it doesn't have to be loud or destructive to be effective. Sometimes, all it takes is a small, deliberate act—a sticker on a statue, a satirical meme, a perfectly timed sign of defiance.

Like a cat swiping a glass of water off the counter, you're sending a message: *This doesn't belong here. And neither do you.*

Fascists will try to frame disruption as unruly, uncivilized, or even dangerous, but let's be honest—they're just embarrassed that you outsmarted them. These are the same people who are probably surrounded by a bunch of people sucking up to them in the hope the power and wealth will rub off. They're not equipped to handle a population full of metaphorical cats who refuse to sit still and behave.

So, embrace the art of deliberate chaos.

Find the symbols of their power—their monuments to mediocrity, their poorly worded propaganda, their deeply unflattering portraits—and give them a little nudge. You don't have to destroy everything; just do enough to make them question whether they've actually got control.

Because at the end of the day, nothing dismantles authoritarianism quite like a well-timed act of defiance.

Be strategic. Be bold. And when the time comes, knock it all over—one paw at a time.

Chapter Four

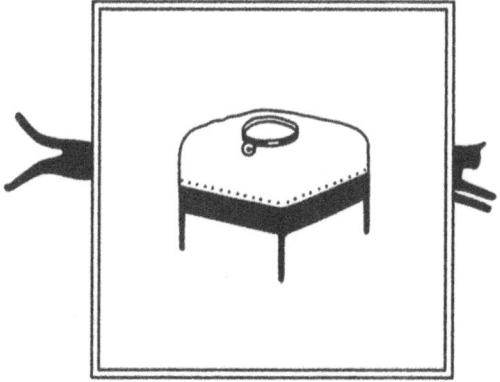

Refuse to Wear Collars

Cats despise collars.
Cats hate *wearing* anything.

Sure, they might look cute for a moment—maybe even Instagram-worthy—but deep down, every cat knows what a collar really represents: control.

The tiny bell jingling with every step? Surveillance.

The snug fit? Domination.

Cats aren't fooled, and neither should we be.

Fascists love collars, metaphorically speaking. They're obsessed with finding ways to make people wear them, often by dressing them up as something "necessary" or even "fashionable." "Oh, it's for your own good!" they chirp, jingling the societal equivalent of a little bell. "Look how it makes you a better citizen!" But much like a cat, you should pause, stare at the collar, and then swat it off the table with a look of utter disdain.

Fascists, let's be honest, are a bit like overzealous dog owners who think every living being needs to be leashed. "Why aren't they wearing their collar?" they demand, clutching their red ball caps. "How will we know where they're going or what they're doing?" The thought of someone walking freely through life, uncollared, untethered, and entirely unpredictable, sends them into a spiral of existential dread.

Cats, however, refuse to be restrained. Even when they grudgingly wear a collar, they'll spend every waking moment plotting its removal.

LESSONS FROM CATS FOR SURVIVING FASCISM

You can practically hear them thinking, *Oh, you believe this little pink band of oppression will stop me?* And that's the energy we need to channel. It's not just about rejecting literal collars—it's about rejecting anything that tries to disguise control as convenience. A bell around your neck so the fascists can always find you? No, thank you.

The funny thing is, fascists aren't even good at making collars look appealing. Their idea of a "cute accessory" is usually something drab and joyless, like a uniform or a badge that screams, "I have no personality!" And yet, they can't understand why people don't line up to wear them. You can almost picture the confusion: "Why don't they like the collar? It's so practical! It's so *efficient*!" Meanwhile, the cats of the world are lounging in their collar-free glory, silently laughing at the absurdity of it all.

The trick is to question every collar you're handed, no matter how harmless it seems. Is it really just a harmless accessory, or is it a way to keep you in line?

Cats know the answer instinctively.

That's why they'd rather dart across busy streets, untagged and unbothered, than let someone slap a leash on them. It's not just about freedom—it's about the principle of the thing.

So, the next time someone tries to slip a metaphorical collar around your neck—whether it's a rule, a label, or a demand for conformity—channel your inner cat. Give them that signature feline look of disdain that says, "I don't think so, moron," and walk away, preferably in the direction of a sunny windowsill where you can nap undisturbed.

Because at the end of the day, life isn't meant to be lived with a bell around your neck and someone else holding the leash. Be uncollared. Be free.

Chapter Five

Perfect the Art of Vanishing

Cats have an uncanny ability to disappear at the exact moment you need them most—or, depending on their mood, when they're about to be blamed for something.

It's not just an instinct; it's an art form.

One second, they're lounging in plain sight, and the next, they've melted into the shadows, leaving you holding an empty treat bag and asking a lot of questions.

This is a skill we should all cultivate, especially when dealing with fascists.

Fascists, for all their bluster, are terrible at dealing with things they can't see. They like to think of themselves as master trackers—patrolling borders, checking lists, and monitoring restrooms—but the reality is closer to a cartoon villain stumbling over their own shoelaces from their own stupid gold sneakers.

Their obsession with control depends entirely on knowing where you are, what you are, what you're doing, and whether you've followed their ridiculous rules about what constitutes "acceptable behavior."

So, when you vanish? They panic. And it's glorious.

Picture it: a fascist, searching desperately for you so they can yell at you and tell you what you're doing (or being) wrong. "They were just here! They're supposed to be in their assigned place/race/face/etc.!"

Meanwhile, you're perched silently on that tiny ledge above the stairs, watching their futile attempts to locate you.

The key is to make your absence as unnerving as possible. Don't just disappear—disappear *strategically*. Leave behind just enough evidence of your presence to make them wonder if you're still nearby, waiting to strike, or if you've already vanished into the ether.

Cats are masters of this psychological warfare.

They don't just leave; they leave on their terms. Maybe they slip into a hidden corner to nap, or maybe they're quietly observing from the shadows, waiting for the perfect moment to pounce. Fascists, on the other hand, have no idea how to cope with such subtlety. They're used to loud, predictable resistance—something they can label, categorize, and, ideally, crush. But a person who knows how to vanish? That's their worst nightmare.

And let's be clear: this isn't about running away. It's about staying one step ahead. A cat doesn't vanish because it's scared—it vanishes because it knows it's smarter than you. Fascists love to puff themselves up as all-seeing and all-knowing, but let's face it: they can barely keep track of their own propaganda or criminal acts, let alone a population of clever, stealthy resisters.

So, practice the art of disappearing. When things get dicey, be the one they can't pin down. Learn to blend in, slip away, and reappear only when it suits you. Maybe you're organizing in the shadows, or maybe you're just enjoying a quiet moment away from their nonsense. Either way, your elusiveness sends a clear message: *You don't own me, and you never will.*

Remember, fascists hate what they can't control, and they can't control what they can't find.

So vanish like a cat who's just heard you open the travel carrier for a trip to the vet—swiftly, silently, and with a hint of smugness. Let them scramble to figure out where you've gone, while you, refreshed and unbothered, prepare your next move.

Because at the end of the day, disappearing isn't about hiding—it's about power. The power to decide when and where you'll be seen. The power to be present on your own terms. And the power to leave fascists standing in the dust, wondering what just happened.

──── Chapter Six ────

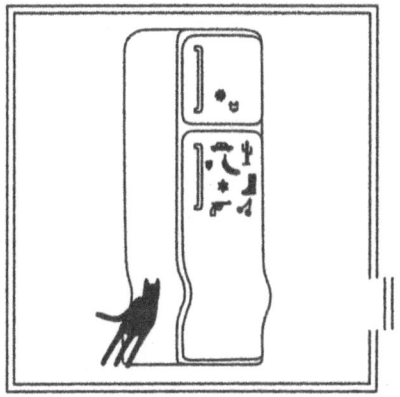

Demand Food with Assertiveness

Cats don't mess around when they're hungry.

They don't sit quietly, hoping someone notices their empty bowl. No, they march straight to the source of the problem and make their demands known—with the kind of ear-piercing yowl that could wake the dead (or at least guilt you into action). Cats know what they need, and they'll make sure you know it too.

It's a lesson we should all take to heart: when something's wrong, speak up. Loudly.

Fascists, naturally, despise this kind of behavior. They rely on people keeping quiet, tolerating injustice, and politely waiting for scraps. "Why can't you just be grateful for what you're given?" they whine, shaking their fists at the metaphorical yowling. But gratitude isn't on the menu when you're starving—for food, for rights, or for basic dignity.

Cats understand this instinctively.

They don't care if you're busy, tired, or pretending not to hear them. If their bowl is empty, you're going to know about it. And if you don't respond right away? They'll double down—circling your ankles, knocking things off the counter, maybe even staring at you with that unsettling, unblinking gaze until you finally cave.

Fascists hate this kind of persistence because it's the opposite of compliance. They prefer silence, the kind where they can hand out half-measures and expect applause. Cats demand more, and so should you.

LESSONS FROM CATS FOR SURVIVING FASCISM

Imagine a fascist dealing with a hungry cat. "Why won't they stop?" they'd mutter, clutching their classified documents. They'd probably try to distract the cat with meaningless platitudes—"Can't you wait a little longer? We're working on a feeding plan! It'll be ready in two weeks!"—only to find that cats, much like the rest of us, don't fall for empty promises. The cat would yowl louder, maybe even throw in a swipe for good measure, and the fascist would crumble under the pressure, retreating to a dark corner to write another banana pants Truth Social post.

The point isn't just to be loud; it's to be unrelenting.

Cats don't quit after one yowl, and neither should you. Keep speaking up, keep demanding what's right, and don't let anyone convince you that you're asking for too much.

You're not.

Whether it's food, fairness, or freedom, you have every right to demand it—preferably in a tone that makes it clear you won't be ignored.

Fascists, for all their posturing, are hilariously bad at handling assertiveness. They think they're the ones in charge, but the moment someone yowls back at them, they're completely thrown off their game. "Wh-wh-why are they so loud?" they'll stammer, as if noise itself is the real threat. Meanwhile, you—channeling your inner cat—are already three steps ahead, making it abundantly clear that you won't stop until your needs are met.

So, the next time you're faced with injustice, don't wait quietly for someone to notice. Speak up. Demand what's right with the kind of confidence only a hungry cat can muster. Be loud. Be persistent. And if the fascists try to drown you out, just yowl louder. After all, if cats

DEMAND FOOD WITH ASSERTIVENESS

can get their way with nothing but a meow and some strategic chaos, imagine what you can do with your voice.

Because at the end of the day, demanding what you need isn't just about survival—it's about principle. It's about refusing to settle for less. And it's about reminding the powers that be that silence may be golden, but yowls get the job done.

———— Chapter Seven ————

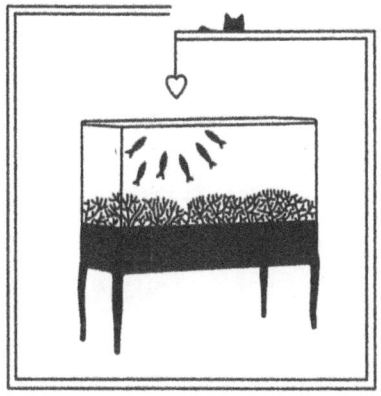

Use Cuteness to Your Advantage

Cats are cunning little masterminds.

One moment, they're on the verge of being scolded for knocking over your favorite mug; the next, they're tilting their head, purring softly, and looking at you with those big, innocent eyes that could melt even the coldest heart.

Suddenly, you're apologizing to *them* for leaving the mug in such an obviously knock-over-able spot. That's the power of cuteness, and it's a skill we should all master.

Fascists, for all their fearmongering and propaganda, are deeply susceptible to charm.

They'd never admit it, of course, but that's because they don't understand how it works. They're too busy puffing out their chests and writing stern policies to notice that you've just dismantled their whole operation with a well-timed smile and a touch of faux innocence. "Wait," they'll mutter, flipping through their rulebook, "are they…allowed to be this endearing?" No, Dear Leader. No one can regulate charisma.

Cats know this better than anyone. When they need allies—or simply a treat they haven't earned—they lean in to their cuteness with the precision of a seasoned diplomat. A soft paw on your knee, a delicate meow, and suddenly you're handing over half your dinner without a second thought. The best part? They don't even have to try that hard.

Fascists, on the other hand, are famously paralyzed by charm.

LESSONS FROM CATS FOR SURVIVING FASCISM

They'd rather spend hours crafting convoluted schemes to enforce loyalty than admit that sometimes a well-placed head tilt is all it takes.

When dealing with oppressive systems, this feline tactic becomes even more powerful. It's hard to vilify someone who seems harmless, adorable even. Channel your inner fluffball when you need to win over skeptics, build alliances, or momentarily distract the powers that be. Lean in with a smile, tilt your metaphorical head, and watch them squirm. Fascists are all about demanding subservience, and nothing disrupts those demands like someone who's too likable to punish.

Imagine a fascist trying to stay angry in the face of unrelenting charm. "But they're breaking the rules!" they'd cry as you flash them your best "Who, me?" expression and follow it up with a well-crafted compliment. Their face would twitch as they tried to resist, but it's no use. You've already disarmed them with the human equivalent of a purr, and now they're questioning their entire psychopathic career choice.

Of course, cuteness alone won't dismantle systems of oppression.

Cats don't rely solely on their charm—they pair it with strategy, persistence, and the occasional well-timed act of rebellion. But cuteness is the gateway, the Trojan horse that gets you through the gates and into the hearts of the people you need on your side.

So, when the situation calls for it, don't hesitate to play the part. Be approachable. Be endearing. Be the kind of person—or cat—who's impossible to resist. Fascists won't know what hit them, and your allies will multiply faster than a litter of kittens.

Because at the end of the day, charm isn't just a survival tactic—it's a weapon. And in a world full of stern-faced authoritarians, sometimes the fluffiest paw packs the hardest punch.

―――― Chapter Eight ――――

Take Over Spaces That Aren't Yours

Cats don't ask permission.

They see an empty box, a chair, or even the middle of your carefully laid-out Monopoly board, and they claim it as their own. No hesitation, no second-guessing. To them, the world is a buffet of opportunities waiting to be taken. And, frankly, that's the energy we need to bring when dealing with power structures—especially ones propped up by fascists.

Fascists love their spaces of power. The big desks, the fancy titles, the platforms they use to spew their nonsense.

But here's the thing: those spaces aren't inherently theirs. They've just planted their flag and hoped no one would challenge them. Enter: you.

Channel your inner cat, walk boldly into their metaphorical boardroom, and take a seat. Preferably one that makes them deeply uncomfortable.

Imagine a fascist walking into a room, only to find you lounging in their chair, cleaning your nails with the kind of relaxed confidence that says, "Oh, were you using this?" Their carefully curated aura of authority would crumble in an instant. "You can't just sit there!" they'd sputter, flipping through their rulebook. But the truth is, you absolutely can. Cats know this.

It's not about asking—it's about occupying.

LESSONS FROM CATS FOR SURVIVING FASCISM

The beauty of this tactic is that it works precisely because fascists are obsessed with territory. They think everything needs a label, a hierarchy, a chain of command.

Cats, of course, reject all of that nonsense. To a cat, if there's an empty space, it's fair game. A chair isn't "reserved"—it's simply unclaimed. And that's how you need to see the spaces of power in the world.

It's not just about taking up physical space, though. It's about inserting yourself into conversations, decision-making processes, and systems that were designed to exclude you. Fascists rely on people staying in their "assigned" roles, not questioning the status quo. But the moment you step into a space they thought was theirs, they have to reckon with your presence. And reckoning isn't their strong suit.

Fascists, bless their rigid little minds, are hilariously bad at improvisation. "But...but you're not supposed to be here!" they'll stammer, as if saying it louder will make you leave. Meanwhile, you're already making yourself comfortable, stretching out like a cat in a sunbeam, and maybe even rearranging a few things for good measure.

The trick is to act like you belong there—because, frankly, you do.

Cats don't second-guess themselves when they hop into your laundry basket or sprawl across your keyboard. They own the moment. They make their presence undeniable. And so should you.

This doesn't mean barging in recklessly. Cats are deliberate. They assess, they wait, and then they move with precision. When you take over a space—whether it's a literal seat at the table or a metaphorical one—do it with purpose. Make it clear that you're not just filling the space; you're reshaping it.

Because at the end of the day, power isn't about who built the

TAKE OVER SPACES THAT AREN'T YOURS

space—it's about who occupies it. And if a cat can turn an Amazon box into a throne, imagine what you can do when you claim the spaces that fascists thought were theirs.

So go ahead. Take the chair, the box, the stage. Claim it with confidence, sit down like you own the place, and don't budge. If they want it back, they'll have to pry it out of your perfectly poised paws.

──────── Chapter Nine ────────

Keep Your Claws Sharp

Even the fluffiest, most cuddly cat has a hidden arsenal of razor-sharp claws, and they aren't afraid to use them.

One moment, they're purring in your lap; the next, they're swiping at you because you dared to pet them in the wrong spot.

"My belly?! Are you insane??!"

Cats don't start fights, but they sure know how to end them. And that's a lesson we should all remember when dealing with fascists.

Fascists, despite their swagger, are terrified of sharp resistance—both literal and metaphorical. They thrive on compliance, preferring a world full of declawed dissenters who can't scratch back. But much like cats, you should never let them think you're defenseless. Sure, you might be soft, approachable, and even charming when it suits you, but if they back you into a corner? That's when the claws come out.

Cats don't swipe indiscriminately; they're precise. They savor the time waiting for conditions to be perfect, then strike with an efficiency that leaves their opponent stunned (and occasionally bleeding).

Fascists, on the other hand, are deeply unprepared for this kind of calculated retaliation. They're used to heavy-handed resistance that they can label and suppress. But a well-timed scratch—a cutting remark, a sharp protest, or a biting comedic commentary posted online? That's the kind of resistance they are woefully unprepared for.

Imagine a fascist trying to corner a metaphorical cat. "Just comply," they'd demand, waving their finger like it's a sword. But instead of rolling over, the cat would casually unsheathe its claws, stretch for dramatic effect, and deliver one precise swipe that eviscerates their finger and sends the fascist's confidence flying across the room. "What just happened?" they'd cry, clutching their bruised egos. What happened, Dear Leader, is that you underestimated the cat.

The key is to keep your claws metaphorically sharp at all times.

Stay informed, stay prepared, and don't let anyone dull your edge. Resistance doesn't have to be constant, but it does need to be effective. A single well-placed strike—at the right policy, the right institution, or the right figurehead—can have more impact than a thousand unfocused jabs.

Cats also remind us that claws are as much about confidence as they are about defense. A cat who knows it can scratch if needed walks differently. It's bold, unbothered, and maybe even a little cocky. Fascists hate that energy. They'd prefer you cower, second-guessing yourself and your ability to fight back. But when you walk into the room with the quiet confidence of a cat who knows its claws are sharp? That's when you become a real threat.

Of course, using your claws doesn't mean abandoning kindness or strategy. Cats are still cuddly, after all—they just know when cuddles aren't enough. The same goes for you. Be approachable, be kind, but don't be afraid to strike when the situation demands it. A well-timed scratch, after all, is worth a thousand words—and often speaks louder than any argument ever could.

So, keep your claws sharp. Stay ready to defend yourself, your values, and your space. And if fascists think they can push you around

KEEP YOUR CLAWS SHARP

without consequence, remind them—swiftly and effectively—that even the softest paws can leave a mark.

Because at the end of the day, resistance isn't about constant aggression—it's about knowing when to act. And when the moment comes, scratch back.

Chapter Ten

Remember You're Always the Boss

Cats don't question their place in the world—they know they're in charge.

Whether they're strutting across your keyboard during a Zoom call or demanding dinner with an imperious meow, cats operate under the unshakable belief that they rule everything the light touches (and plenty of things it doesn't). This confidence doesn't waver, no matter the circumstances. And that's a lesson we should all take to heart, especially when facing fascists.

Fascists, despite their chest-thumping bravado, are deeply insecure.

They project power because they know they don't truly have it—not where it matters, anyway. They thrive on making you feel small, on convincing you that they're the boss and you're just a powerless bystander in their grand scheme. But here's the secret: they only win if you let them. Cats, of course, would never let them.

Picture a fascist trying to exert control over a cat. "You can't sit there!" they'd bark, pointing to an off-limits chair. The cat, naturally, would hop onto the chair, stare at them for a moment, and then slowly begin licking its nether regions, radiating an air of *Oh, I didn't hear you over the sound of me not caring, and by the way, have you seen my amazingly clean butt?*

This isn't just defiance—it's dignity. Cats don't give up their autonomy for anyone, and neither should you.

LESSONS FROM CATS FOR SURVIVING FASCISM

When the odds seem stacked against you, that's when channeling your inner cat becomes most important. Cats don't dwell on how outnumbered they might be or how big the dog chasing them looks. They carry themselves with unshakable confidence, because they know their worth isn't dictated by external forces. A fascist may try to loom over you with their rules and regulations, but maintaining your dignity—walking tall, speaking clearly, and acting with purpose—is the ultimate form of resistance.

Fascists don't want you to have unbridled confidence. It makes them nervous, flustered, even a little sweaty. They'll try to undermine it with intimidation tactics, but much like a cat being shooed off a counter, you should respond by hopping back up with even more attitude. "Oh, this space? Yeah, I'm still here. Thanks for checking."

The beauty of acting like the boss isn't about arrogance—it's about refusing to shrink yourself. Cats don't question their right to occupy space, and neither should you. Speak your mind, assert your presence, and carry yourself as though you own the room, even if it's filled with fascists who'd rather you didn't exist.

Confidence isn't just a shield—it's a weapon.

And if fascists try to knock you down, take another cue from cats: land on your feet, shake it off, and continue ruling your world like nothing happened. They'll be too busy scratching their heads to figure out how you did it.

So, remember: you're always the boss. Not them, not their rules, not their systems of control. Walk through life with the swagger of a cat who knows the world is theirs to command. Let your dignity shine, your confidence radiate, and your belief in your own authority become the kind of quiet revolution that no fascist can ever extinguish.

Because at the end of the day, the boss isn't the one who shouts the loudest—they're the one who knows, deep down, that they never stopped being in charge.

Chapter Eleven

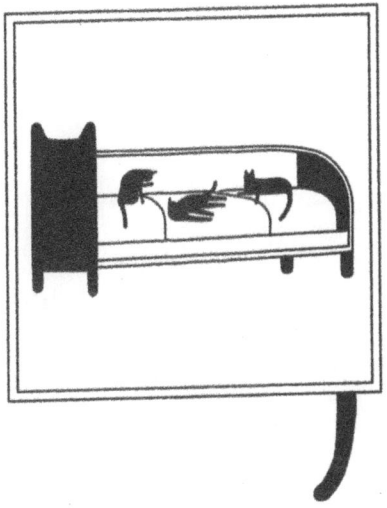

Look After Your Pride

Cats may act like lone operators—aloof, self-sufficient, and occasionally too cool for their own good—but anyone who's spent enough time with them knows better. Beneath that "I don't need anyone" exterior is a creature who knows the value of a community. They groom each other, share sunny spots, and occasionally (begrudgingly) team up to take down bigger threats, like the vacuum cleaner or that bird that keeps taunting them through the window.

Fascists, on the other hand, don't understand the concept of care. Their whole worldview depends on keeping people isolated, pitted against one another, and too preoccupied with survival to notice that the real enemy is the one handing out collars and MAGA caps. But here's the thing about cats: they don't just look after themselves—they look after their pride.

When a kitten is too small to fend for itself, older cats step in. When one cat takes a swipe at the food bowl, others join in to make sure everyone gets their share (even if it's accompanied by some side-eye). This isn't weakness—it's strength. Cats know that their survival isn't just about sharp claws and stealthy moves; it's about watching out for each other, sharing resources, and sticking together when it matters most.

As you channel your inner cat—knocking things over, yowling for justice, and sharpening your claws—don't forget to look out for the other members of your pride. Groom each other, metaphorically speaking.

LESSONS FROM CATS FOR SURVIVING FASCISM

Share strategies. Offer a sunny spot to someone who's been in the shadows for too long. And when the time comes to face the metaphorical vacuum cleaner of oppression, go in as a team.

Fascists can't handle solidarity. They bank on division and discord, assuming that people (and cats) are too selfish to cooperate. But the moment they see a room full of uncollared, well-fed, razor-sharp individuals working together, they lose their footing. "Wait," they'll mutter, "aren't they supposed to be fighting over the chair? Why are they sharing it?" Because, Dear Leader, we understand what you don't: taking care of each other is the ultimate power move.

So, whether you're licking wounds, sharing resources, or simply offering a comforting paw to someone in need, remember that caring for your pride isn't just kindness—it's strategy. A well-cared-for pride is a force to be reckoned with, the kind of collective power that no fascist Project 20-whatever can predict.

Because at the end of the day, being a cat isn't just about surviving—it's about thriving. And no cat thrives alone.

Now go forth, proud, uncollared, and sharp-clawed, and take care of each other. The pride is stronger together, and the fascists? Well, they don't stand a chance.